MACHINE LEARNING

THE 10 CLASSIFIERS IN PYTHON

Yeeshtdevisingh Hosanee

Acknowledgement

Special thanks goes to Mrs Suryamball Hosanee, the mother of the author, for her tremendous input during the whole publication process of this book. The author wishes to also thank her sister, Kedarshinisingh Hosanee, Dr Panchoo, Priya, Kavish, her friends and colleagues for their continuous encouragement in relation to the publication of this book. A special thanks Mrs Lakshmi for her favourable recommendations during the publication of the book.

First Edition, 2023
ISBN: 9789392274893
Publisher: National Academic Press, Chennai, India
Distribution in India: SHANTI BOOKS LIBRARY BOOK SUPPLIER & DISTRIBUTOR, Chennai, Tamil Nadu 600005
Outside India by online distribution with Imprint: YEEHOS

Table of Contents

List of Tables

Table 1 The ML Classification Chart**Error!   Bookmark   not defined.**

Introduction

This book is written for students who want to get started with Machine Learning (ML) concepts. The programming language used in this book is the Python language.

A prior programming knowledge would definitely help in understanding the different syntax in the Python Language. Nevertheless, even though you do not have any prior programming knowledge, understanding the rationale is clearly explained in the book and you will gain in knowledge.

The book has two main chapters: the theoretical and the practical chapter. In chapter 1, you will understand why machine learning exists, the difference between data science and machine learning, the different areas of machine learning, difference between supervised and unsupervised learning, the classifiers in supervised learning and history of machine learning till date.

In the practical section, which is in chapter 2, you will be presented with a typical example whereby a university admission program needs to be developed with Machine Learning (ML) techniques. To be admitted successfully for a course at the university, the program requires students to have all, at least 5 marks in each of the following three academic subjects: English, French and Mathematics.

Ten subsequent chapters will follow. In each chapter, you will be introduced to a different ML technique, the classifiers. You will use each classifier to develop the same ML admission program to predict if a new student would be sufficiently eligible to enrol for a course in the university. The ten classifiers are: Logistic Regression (LR), Naïve Bayes (NB), Gaussian Process (GP), K-Nearest Neighbors (KNN), Quadratic Discriminant Analysis (QDA), decision tree, AdaBoost, Random Forest, Support Vector Machine (SVM) and multilayer perceptron (MTP).

Once the basic concepts of Machine Learning (ML) have been acquired, you as a learner, will be able to proceed with more advanced concepts in Machine Learning (ML) and Artificial Intelligence (AL).

1.1. What is Machine Learning?

Machine Learning (ML) is a branch of the Artificial Intelligence (AI) and the latter is a branch of Computer Science (CS). Hence, Machine Learning is a subset of the field of Computer Science.

Machine Learning (ML) is one field where a lot of mathematical equations are being used in statistical models, which have all the aim, to predict a value or some values based on some known or unknown conditions.

These models used a series of sequential steps to achieve a goal. These set of steps are known as ML algorithms or ML techniques. ML algorithms or ML techniques are today being used to achieve pattern recognition and prediction goals. For instance, in banks, ML is being used to check for eligibility of clients of a loan. Card fraud detection is also possible with ML techniques. It is also being used for school or university admission process to check eligibility of students before enrolment process can take place.

However, these ML techniques would not work without any data consumption by machines. A machine can be a laptop, a computer, a mobile phone, a radio or even a washing machine. Manipulating and analysing these different data by these ML techniques is possible with Machine Learning (ML).

1.2. ML techniques learnt in this book

Ten ML techniques, also known as ten classifiers, will be taught in this book. They are: Logistic Regression, Naives Bayes (NB), Gaussian Process Classifier (GPC), K-Nearest Neighbors (KNN), Quadratic Discriminant Analysis (QDA), Decision Tree, AdaBoost, Random Forest, Support Vector Machine (SVM) and Multiple Perceptron (MTP).

These ten techniques have all a common goal to predict if a new student is eligible to enrol for a university course. With each technique taught, a different ML program would be developed to achieve this goal. At the end of this book, a total of ten ML programs will be presented to you.

In each program, for every student, the marks of three academic subjects should be provided to it. The subjects are English, French and Mathematics. In each program, the past admission records would be analysed by the ML techniques to give the prediction.

The programming language chosen to develop ML programs in this book is the Python language.

1.3. Types of ML models, prediction and probability

An ML model must develop a pattern recognition ability to be able to predict a value. Today to identify these patterns, we have two categories of model to describe the ML techniques. We can classify them into structural dynamics and operational dynamics.

The parametric and non-parametric models form part of the structural dynamics. The discriminant and generative models form part of the operational dynamics.

Structural dynamics are concerned about how the structure affects a model and operational dynamics are concerned about how the organisation of the content will affect the model.

In a parametric model, the number of parameters will influence the model. No matter how many data records you add to your parametric model, the number of parameters would not change.

However, in a non-parametric model, if you add new data records to your model, you can change the number of parameters. The flexibility benefit in a non-parametric model, allows pattern recognition to new data and unknown scenarios, to be more effective in comparison to a using parametric model. Complex problems are usually solved with non-parametric models and smaller problems size are solved with parametric models.

An ML model categorised either as a parametric or non-parametric model, would be needing an operational dynamics model to organise the data records and analyse them. Either the discriminant or generative model would combine with one of the structural dynamics models to be able to create a predicted value. A prediction with an ML model, is a process to estimate a value which looks nearly or true to the actual value. To be able to predict, we use these models which uses a lot of probability formula. A probability is a process which find a way to compute the predicted value.

A discriminant model uses conditional probability principles, and a generative model uses joint probability principles. With conditional probability, your data is selective. You are not examining the whole population of your sample. With joint probability, you perform a series of multiplication and often you will use the whole population to find a probability for your prediction.

For instance, if you have the choice to flight from France to Dubai, among many, you find three suitable options: You can have a direct flight to Dubai or you can transit through Italy or you can transit also through Austria. You consider distance and price of air ticket as two parameters in your selection choice. You did not consider the speed of plane as one of your parameters.

With a simple mathematical division you can easily see the difference. We will fractionise our three choises to understand its impact in ML predictions.

- If we give a score of 1 for each choice options, we have a total of three scores to be considered.
- In the case where you have not considered the speed as one selection criterion, your calculation would be 2/2 = 1
- In the case where you have considered the speed as one selection criterion, your division would fractionize into 2/3 = 0.67.

In the field of Mathematics, with regards to fractions, a value which is less than 1, is considered to have some accuracy error to the true value. If the final value after fractionising two numbers equals to 1, this is the best choice you can make.

If you do not consider speed as one parameter, your choice will be biased, and you would consider the value it the best choice. You need to cater for all the three parameters in your estimation: distance, cost, and speed.

Discriminant models are more biased than generative models because they are selective in nature. When you did not consider the speed as one of your parameter, you have been selective in a similar way to a discriminant model. However, being selective works well with smaller problems because the models know its boundaries. For our flight example, a discriminant model would work well if the conditions were all flights should be small in size. Hence, speed is not a concern. The condition (boundary) for the discriminant model would be all plane size should be small.

In the case of a generative model, no boundary is present. The model learns by itself and distribute the data accordingly. It is more challenging to control the different data created but works best with complex problems. In the case where you will consider the three criteria: distance, cost and speed, for your choice, an generative ML model would take more time to compute to fine the optimum solution for you because they have more variations in the data (no conditions to rely on).

To summarise, an ML model can have the following characteristics:
1) Being a parametric model with discriminant properties
2) Being a parametric model with generative properties
3) Being a non-parametric model with discriminant properties
4) Being a non-parametric model with generative properties

1.4. Types of data

As Machine Learning relies a lot on data values, it is important to understand the types of data that exist today. There are four types of data: nominal, ordinal, discrete and continuous data.

Nominal and Ordinal data are qualitative in nature. Discrete and Continuous data are quantitative. Qualitative data are categorical and quantitative data are numerical.

➢ Nominal data are categorical, but do not need to follow an order. For example, gender can either be male or female, and marital status of a person can vary from single, divorced or married. These values do not have any order preference on each other.

➢ However, for ordinal data, there is an order preference. For example, the economic status of a country can be low, medium or high. These three data values have a meaning of importance to define the economic status.

➢ Discrete data is one digit which explains a situation, e.g. the total number of students present in a class or days in a week.

➢ Continuous data can vary from situation to situation and can even have decimal values, e.g., height or weight of a person.

1.5. Difference between Data Science and ML

Data Science is another area in the Computer Science (SC) field. It is concerned with understanding the data source coming from where till the data has been given a meaning. Data Science does use many ML techniques to be able to give meaning to the data. Giving meaning to the data is possible with ML models and techniques. However, ML scope is not concerned in about the amount of data to input in the model, the consistency and integrity of the data in the model. Managing the data from source till the end, is a process that is performed in the Data Science field.

1.6. Relationship construction in Mathematics

Let us take a real-life situation for you to understand what makes a relationship in mathematics. Suppose a person when he eats one apple per day, he can walk one kilometre (1 km) in distance. If he eats two apples, he can walk two kilometres (2 km). If he has eaten three apples, he can walk three kilometres (3 km).

As you can see, as the number of apples is incrementing by one value, the number of kilometres does also increase by one value. This kind of relationship between number of apples eaten and the number of kilometres in distance, where the increase in distance is constantly changing with the increase in number of apples eaten by the same value each time, is known as a linear relationship.

In the field of Mathematics, a linear relationship is normally defined with an equation: Y=mX + C, where, in our example, Y is the number of kilometres to walk through, X is the number of apples eaten, m can be another factor which influences the distance to cover. For instance, m can be a variable to distinguish an action that happens either in the morning or at night.

If the person walks in the morning, he has more energy compared if he walks in the evening. The m-value can indicate the type of energy he has. A positive m-value such as +1 can be given if the person walks in the morning. If the person walks in the evening, the m-value can be -1.

The value of C in a linear equation, is a value which always equals to Y, when X is 0. In our example, the person walks only after having eaten an apple, not in between. In case, the person already walked two kilometres and then decided to eat one apple, C would be a value for the extra two kilometres that he has already been covered before eating an apple (as a starting point).

Now given that a person, when he eats one apple, he can walk one kilometre (1 km). When he eats two apples, he can walk three kilometres (3 km) and when he eats three apples, he can walk six kilometres (6 km). In this example, the number of kilometres is not increasing by the same value. When the person eats three apples, he can walk two kilometres more than when he has eaten one apple. He can walk an extra of three kilometres, only if he eats three apples. When a final value, such as the distance in kilometres, is not increasing constantly with a constant input (the number of apples), this relationship is known as a non-linear one.

1.7. Bias in statistics

In the field of ML, the term bias or weight is interchangeably being used. Bias or weight is used to reduce accuracy problems related to data values.
The problem, not only in ML, but in real-life, when we analyse data values with smaller gap in between, we cannot determine how close the new data are to the existing data values.

If we take a look at our previous example, where a person can walk one kilometre (1 km) when he has eaten one apple, he can walk three kilometre (3 km) when he has eaten two apples and he can walk six kilometres (6 km) when he has eaten three apples. Now let say, the person has eaten two and a half apple (2.5), predicting whether he will be able to walk close to 3 km or 6 km is difficult because the gap difference between six- and three-kilometres distance is small.

To make accurate prediction and see the gap difference between data, bias is used. A bias of 100, would multiply the actual values by 100 and result into 100, 300 and 600 for 1,3 and 6 km respectively. If a person eats one, two and three apples respectively, you can clearly see that 300 and 600 has a large gap.

In a similar way, machine can give us more accurate values when bias are introduced in mathematical equations in the different ML models.

1.8. Areas of Machine Learning

Frank Rosenblatt from Cornell University initiate the Machine Learning concepts. He set up a group of people to build a machine for recognising letters of different alphabets (Fradkov, 2020). Perceptron is the name given to the machine which was built. The machine built could convert analog signals to discreate ones. The machine model of imitating the human nervous system was close to the models developed in cognitive psychology. That model, they name it the artificial neural networks (ANN), which is one concept in machine learning (Fradkov, 2020). Since, then many other concepts have been introduced.

Machine Learning (ML) has four core functionalities: Supervised Learning, Unsupervised Learning, Reinforcement Learning and Semi-supervised Learning.

Deep Learning is a subset of Machine Learning where the models such as Neural Network or Artificial Neural Network (ANN) are being used.

1.9. Supervised Learning

Supervised Learning is about training a program on past values so that the program can see a pattern and predict new values. For example, in real-life if you bet your cash on a football game, you always look at the previous performance of the players and then you predict your new score. In ML, a program on a machine, will be predicting the score based on some pre-conditions you have given, the past data. These ML techniques used to perform this kind of prediction on past information, is known as the Supervised Learning techniques.

The latter can further be categorised into two other types: Classification and Regression.

Classification techniques are methods which will predict discrete values, e.g., true or false.
Regression techniques are methods which will predict continuous values, i.e., the weight of a person can be either 54.5 kg or 67.7 kg.

1.10.   Unsupervised Learning

Unsupervised Learning is another technique in ML which uses unlabelled data and categorise the data. It can use both past data and real-time data to identify a pattern. Moreover, there exist two types of unsupervised learning: clustering and association.

Unsupervised Learning usually requires a threshold to determine if the prediction is correct or not. Again, if you wish to bet your cash on the football game, you do not wish to look at the players' performance. You just want to give your predicted score based on the current betting odds values. These odds act as a threshold to your prediction. You will win only if the odds are very good. Same thing happens in an unsupervised learning, you have a threshold value, and your data are categorised according to the threshold value.

1.11.   Reinforcement Learning

Reinforcement has root from the behavioural psychology where a program is not aware of any expected values. It takes inputs and whatever results it got; it tries to see its optimum path to be inputted in another goal.

Like unsupervised learning, reinforcement Learning also works with unlabelled data. However, it has a rewarding function in its goal. For example, if you want to predict five subsequent football games, you can wait for the previous one to finish for predicting in the next game. In case you win the previous one and you have been rewarded in cash, you will be happy to invest your money in the next one. This is reinforcement. You are analysing information from your previous wins to reinforce the winning possibility of your subsequent matches.

1.12.   Semi-supervised Learning

In a semi-supervised learning, a small portion of data are labelled In a similar way to supervised learning. But it also combines these small portions of data with unlabelled data to train a predictive model. For instance, when we bet a football game, we will not go through hundred (100) games to review players' performance. We will be selective in our analysis. We shall use supervised learning technique to review five games and then use unsupervised technique to use the odds as a threshold, combined these two techniques together to get a final predicted score for the upcoming football match.

1.13. Deep Learning

Deep Learning is a subset of Machine Learning where the models such as Neural Network or Artificial Neural Network (ANN) are being used. It attempts to imitate the human neural network in the brain. In treasure map games, when a person wants to look for an object, he will move in a forward direction and when he cannot find its route to the treasure, that person returns to an initial point to start over again the quest. Moving forward and going backward are similar actions that happen in Deep Learning. Different data will be analysed by deep learning models and determine if they must move backward or forward to decrease errors and increase accuracy level.

1.14.   Programming languages for AI applications

Today, different programming languages such as Python, Java, visual basic or C++, do have Machine Learning (ML) functionalities. Most of these languages, require you to additionally install these ML functionalities, beside the core functionalities they offer you.

The terminology we use in the field of computer science for these group of functionalities, is known as either a package or a library. The latter consists of many modules having different functionalities.

These modules are also known as classes, a term used in Object Oriented Programming (OOP).

1.15.   Python programming language

Python, a high-level programming language, was designed in 1991 by Guido van Rossum. A high-level programming language consists of alphabetical letters and punctuation marks. A low-level programming language consists of only a series of 0's and 1's, compared to high-level language where the language is human readable.

1.16.   Installation steps for ML programs

Spyder application has been used to test the different Python codes of this book. This tool comes within the installation of Anaconda application set up. If you are comfortable with other types of ML tool, you are encouraged to use any other.

You will have to download Anaconda from its official website. Anaconda is an application tool having many artificial intelligence and ML packages. You can connect on anaconda.org website for more information. The scikit-learn package is important for ML techniques.

To write ML applications, use the Spyder application to write and save your codes, but use the "Anaconda Prompt" to run the codes.

To install any AI packages, use the "Anaconda Powershell Prompt". The following commands have been useful for the installation process:

> pip install scikit-learn

Ten examples, each explaining one ML classifier with their respective Python codes are shown in chapter 2. The expected result and a descriptive explanation of the steps to follow are also provided for every example given.

Overview of the 10 examples

The following section gives an overview of each example:

Example 1: Logistic Regression

The different characteristics of the Logistic Regression (LR) is explained. The mathematical formula used in LR is also shared. The goal of the student admission prediction model is explained in this example. The codes in Python is explained for implementing the prediction model.

The difference between an ML program and a traditional programming development is explained.

Example 2: Naïve Bayes

The difference between Naïve Bayes model and Bayes theorem is explained. The difference between Naives Bayes model and Logistic Regression is also shown. The python codes have ben explained.

Example 3: Gaussian Process Classifier

The origin of Gaussian Process (GP) was mentioned. The advantages of having Gaussian Process rather than Logistic and Naïve Bayes have also been explained. The different python codes to implement the admission program with the GP model has been shown.

Example 4: K-Nearest Neighbors (KNN)

The origin of the K-Nearest Neighbours algorithm, its advantages and the codes to implement the KNN in Python have been clearly demonstrated.

Example 5: Quadratic Discriminant Analysis (QDA)

The difference between Linear and Quadratic Discriminant Analysis was explained. The different codes to implement the admission eligibility program QDA in Python were also explained.

Example 6: Decision Tree

The origin of the decision tree algorithm, its advantages and also the codes to implement the admission eligibility program with the decision tree model have been clearly demonstrated.

Example 7: AdaBoost

The origin of the decision tree algorithm, its advantages and also the codes to implement the admission eligibility program with the AdaBoost tree model have been clearly demonstrated.

Example 8: Random Forest

A comparison of the Random Forest and decision tree is given.

Its advantages and the codes to implement the admission eligibility program with the decision random forest model have been clearly demonstrated.

Example 9: Support Vector Machine (SVM)

The origin of the SVM algorithm, its advantages and the codes to implement the admission eligibility program with the SVM model have been clearly demonstrated.

Example 10: Multiple Perceptron (MTP)

The origin of the MTP algorithm, its advantages and also the codes to implement the admission eligibility program with the MTP model have been presented.

Example 1: Logistic Regression classifier

Explanation

The word "regression" can be confusing to think that Logistic Regression solves only regression problem. A logistic regression can be used both for regression and classification problems. In case of regression problems, continuous data can be obtained for the expected and predicted values (Y-values). In the case of solving a classification problem, the data are categorical, either true or false. If numerical values are used to represent the expected/predicted values, they are usually in binary form with values 0 and 1.

The logistic regression evaluates a non-linear relationship between an input (X) and an output (Y). Its mathematical formula is given as: $Y = e^{(b0 + b1X)}/(1+e^{(b0+b1X)})$, where X is an input value, Y is the predicted value, b_0 is the bias or intercept term and b1 is the coefficient for the single input value of X. But in Python, when you work with Scikit-Learn libraries, these formulae are not presented to the developer. The libraries catered for the formula so that you as a developer you are focused more on the data and prediction processes.

In the example given in this book, we will analyse past students who attempted to enrol for a seat in a university.

Students who had marks greater than four in all three academic subjects: English, French and Mathematics, were admitted successfully admitted for a course at the University and they were marked with status value "Yes" in the record system. Unsuccessful students who could not get a seat, were marked with status value "No" in the university record system.

The machine learning program needs to analyse these past data values to predict if new students can successfully enrolled to the university. The marks for the three academic subjects: English, French and Mathematics, needs to be given for the ML program to analyse and give a prediction.

The following set of codes shows the usage of the LR classifier to check eligibility of new students to be admitted to the university. The steps to carry out for the program development and the output on the screen of the admin officer, are further described.

```python
import pandas as pd

from sklearn.linear_model import LogisticRegression

from sklearn.model_selection import train_test_split

from sklearn.metrics import accuracy_score


#list of headers/columns
headers=['ENGLISH','FRENCH', 'MATHEMATICS', 'ADMITTED']


# row values
values=[[1, 2, 3, 'No'],
        [3, 4, 5, 'No'],
        [5, 6, 7, 'Yes'],
        [7, 8, 9, 'Yes'],
        [1, 2, 6, 'No'],
        [1, 2, 8, 'No'],
        [3, 5, 5, 'No'],
        [8, 7, 8, 'Yes'],
        [7, 7, 7, 'Yes'],
        [8, 2, 5, 'No']]


#Create the frame to include all data and headers
matrix=pd.DataFrame(data=values,columns=headers)



#Separate Target Variable and Predictor Variables
```

```python
cause=['ENGLISH','FRENCH', 'MATHEMATICS']
effect='ADMITTED'


x=matrix[cause].values
y=matrix[effect].values


#Split the data into training and testing set


X_train, X_test, y_train, y_test = train_test_split(x, y, test_size=1)


#builiding classifier model
cmodel = LogisticRegression()


#Creating the model on Training Data
cmodel=cmodel.fit(X_train,y_train)


#input marks for  english, french and mathematics
X_test=[[7,6,8]]


# the predicted result based on the inputs
y_pred=cmodel.predict(X_test)
```

```python
#print values to the user
print("-------------")
print("Current student's marks as follows:")
for i in range(len(X_test[0])):
    print(str(i+1)+"."+headers[i],"=", X_test[0][i], " marks")


print("------result-------")
if y_pred[0]=="Yes":
   print("Student will be admitted to the university.")
else:
   print("Student will not be admitted to the university.")



print('Accuracy: ',accuracy_score(y_test,y_pred))



import matplotlib.pyplot as plt
plt.plot(X_test, y_pred);
plt.show()
```

Figure 1 Logistic Regression program

Thirteen steps have been taken to build eligibility program with the LR classifier:

Step 1: Import the different packages needed for ML functionalities.

`import pandas as pd`, used to create a matrix for the data rows and headers

`from sklearn.linear_model import LogisticRegression`, used to import LogisticRegression function from Python ML libraries.

`from sklearn.model_selection import train_test_split`, used to split the matrix into x and y values.

`from sklearn.metrics import accuracy_score`, used to calculate the accuracy between testing values and predicted values.

Step 2: The goal of the program is to analyse past data such as marks and admission status in a university to predict if new students can be enrolled successfully to the university. For the ML application to analyse, past enrolment data of the University should be analysed. These data should consist four main information: English, French and mathematics marks, and corresponding admission status for each student attempting to admit at the university in the past.

A matrix consisting of rows and columns will be created. You will have to define the headers for each column at this stage. Assign these values to an array "headers". "ENGLISH", "FRENCH", "MATHEMATICS" and "ADMITTED" are the four column headers for the matrix. "ENGLISH", "FRENCH" and "MATHEMATICS" will keep marks for each existing student at the University and "ADMITTED" will keep the status of the student if he has successfully or unsuccessfully been admitted.

```
headers=['ENGLISH','FRENCH', 'MATHEMATICS', 'ADMITTED']
```

Step 3: For each header/column you mentioned in step 2, you will have to input their corresponding values in an array. Remember, as we are dealing with classification problem, our last values should be either true or false. In this case, the last column "AMITTED" consists of values between "Yes" and "No" only.

```
values=[[1, 2, 3, 'No'],
        [3, 4, 5, 'No'],
        [5, 6, 7, 'Yes'],
        [7, 8, 9, 'Yes'],
        [1, 2, 6, 'No'],
        [1, 2, 8, 'No'],
```

[3, 5, 5, 'No'],
[8, 7, 8, 'Yes'],
[7, 7, 7, 'Yes'],
[8, 2, 5, 'No']]

Step 4: Convert all values to 0 and 1 for ML to analyse the data. The two variables "cause" and "effect" have been declared for temporary used. They hold the format required to determine which values from the matrix "values" are x-values and which one among them is the y-predicted value.

```
cause=['ENGLISH','FRENCH', 'MATHEMATICS']
effect='ADMITTED'
```

Step 5: convert all the values to 0 and 1.

```
x=matrix[cause].values
y=matrix[effect].values
```

Step 6: A matrix when given to an ML program can be split into two categories of data: train and test data. In our example, we have 10 rows. The ML program can consider the first nine rows as its past data and consider the last row as the new test data. This is achieved with the parameter:

test_size=1. If you wish that the ML program, does consider three rows out of ten rows as your test values, you will have to change the parameter value accordingly as such: test_size=3.

The past data is considered as the trained data, and the new test data is the one you have selected to get a predicted value. With Known X-values in your trainning data, the ML program knows the expected Y-values from the same train data (the first nine rows of your matrix). With a known X-value in your test data, the ML program would now predict an unknown Y-value for you.

Although the data has been split into trainning and testing values, the y_test and X_test values in the codes, were not used because we explicitly change the X_test values at a later stage in the program with the value 7,6 and 8 as shown below:
X_test=[[7,6,8]]

In the codes, the y_test value retrieved, helps only to determine the accuracy between new predicted Y-value and y_test value.
Split the different values into train and test values with the following line of codes:

X_train, X_test, y_train, y_test = train_test_split(x, y, test_size=l)

Step 7: Call and build the classifier model. The one chosen here is the logisticRegression. As our y-values are either true or false, the classifier model in Python will already understand that we are dealing with a classification problem.


```
#builiding classifier model
cmodel = LogisticRegression()
```


Step 8: Pass your trained values of X and Y (the nine rows of your matrix) to the classifier model.


```
cmodel=cmodel.fit(X_train,y_train)
```


Step 9: Input x-values which needs to be predicted. In this case, you want to predict the status, when a student has 7 marks in English, 6 marks in French and 8 marks in Mathematics. You can input the values in an array as such:


```
X_test=[[7,6,8]]
```

Step 9: Pass your three marks (7,6,8) for your three subjects to the model to predict the status of admission for the new student.

```
y_pred=cmodel.predict(X_test)
```

Step 10: Pass your three marks (7,6,8) for your three subjects to the model to predict the status of admission for the new student.

```
y_pred=cmodel.predict(X_test)
```

Step 11: Print the result on the screen for the user. List all the marks inputted to the system for prediction.

```
for i in range(len(X_test[0])):
    print(str(i+1)+"."+headers[i],"=", X_test[0][i], " marks")
```

Step 12: Determine if the student can be admitted or not based on the Y-value predicted. As y_pred is an array, you will have to verify the first value of y_pred with y_pred[0].

```
if y_pred[0]=="Yes":
   print("Student will be admitted to the university.")
else:
```

print("Student will not be admitted to the university.")

Step 13: This step is optional in case you would want to check the accuracy of the Y-Predicted value with the past Y-Values. As the Y-Predicted value is a single value, we need only one value from the past dataset to perform the comparison. Remember earlier, we did a split of one row for the test values with: X_train, X_test, y_train, y_test = train_test_split(x, y, test_size=1).

The splitting helped to fetch one value for "y_test" and allowed us to perform the accuracy_score to get the accuracy on how close the predicted Y-value is to the y_test value.

print('Testing Set Evaluation Accuracy: ',accuracy_score(y_test,y_pred))

The following output is shown on the user's screen when the input marks were: 7, 6 and 8. The ML program successfully identified the student as a potential student to the university and print the message *"Student will be admitted to the university"* on the screen.

```
-------------
Current student's marks as follows:
1.ENGLISH = 7  marks
2.FRENCH = 6  marks
3.MATHEMATICS = 8  marks
------result-------
Student will be admitted to the university.
Accuracy:  1.0
```

Figure 2 Successful admission with LR

Unsuccessful admission with LR

The following output is shown on the user's screen when the input marks were: 7, 6 and 2. The ML program identified the student as being ineligible for the admission process. The following message was printed on screen: *Student will not be admitted to the university.*

```
-------------

Current student's marks as follows:

1.ENGLISH = 7 marks

2.FRENCH = 6 marks

3.MATHEMATICS = 2 marks

------result-------

Student will not be admitted to the university.

Accuracy:  0.0
```

Figure 3 Not eligible for admission with LR

Compare traditional and ML programming

The difference between traditional programming and ML can be shown in the next figure. Three marks are inputted to the system with values 7,6 and 8, same as the one we have seen in Figure 1, of this book.

In traditional programming, you can compare the individual mark inputted in the Python codes itself, with the different if and else statements (conditional statements). Today, machine learning allows the program to train itself and knows when to have these "if" and "else" conditions, without the developer needing to type these logic. During the coding process, the developer focuses more on the functional side of a problem he wants to solve rather than focuses more on the technicities of the programming language. The program is learning from a set of data provided. Therefore, machine learning depends on a lot of data to train the reasoning skills of a program.

```
marks1=7

marks2=6

marks3=8


if (marks1>4) & (marks2>4) & (marks3>4):

   print("Student will  be admitted to the university.")

else:

   print("Student will not be admitted to the university.")
```

Figure 4 Comparison in traditional programming

Practical questions

Predict the admission status for students with the following English, French and Mathematics set of marks:

1. 1,7,3
2. 7,7,7
3. 8,8,8
4. 9,2,3
5. 7,3,4

Example 2: Naïve Bayes classifier

Explanation

Naives Bayes classifier is a prediction model (Berrar, 2018; Lewis, 1998; Saritas & Yasar, 2019). Not to confuse with Bayes Theorem which is a result of an equation (Berrar, 2018; Lewis, 1998; Saritas & Yasar, 2019). Naives Bayes models do use some of the principles of Bayes Theorem, but it also uses other principles from other theories. Naives Bayes is a generative model which encourage joint probability for the whole sample population (using multiplication). Whereas Bayes Theorem uses the conditional probability with restricted sample population.

Compared to Logistic Regression which uses discriminant model and caters for outliers, Naïve Bayes is a generative model, which is more about to create errors if not properly handle. Discriminative models separate groups of data by using conditional probability, not making any assumptions about individual data points. The word "Naives" has been given to the model because it assumes all input values (X) are independent of each other, unrealistic for real data. But the technique was proven effective for very large complex problems. The following codes show how Naïve Bayes was implemented in our University admission process to check for eligibility of new students to register for a course:

```python
# import python libraries

import pandas as pd

from sklearn.model_selection import train_test_split

from sklearn.metrics import accuracy_score

from sklearn.naive_bayes import GaussianNB

#list of headers/columns

headers=['ENGLISH','FRENCH', 'MATHEMATICS', 'ADMITTED']


# row values

values=[[1, 2, 3, 'No'],

        [3, 4, 5, 'No'],

        [5, 6, 7, 'Yes'],

        [7, 8, 9, 'Yes'],

        [1, 2, 6, 'No'],

        [1, 2, 8, 'No'],

        [3, 5, 5, 'No'],

        [8, 7, 8, 'Yes'],

        [7, 7, 7, 'Yes'],

        [8, 2, 5, 'No']]


#Create the frame to include all data and headers

matrix=pd.DataFrame(data=values,columns=headers)



#Separate Target Variable and Predictor Variables
```

```python
cause=['ENGLISH','FRENCH', 'MATHEMATICS']
effect='ADMITTED'


x=matrix[cause].values
y=matrix[effect].values


#Split the data into training and testing set


X_train, X_test, y_train, y_test = train_test_split(x, y, test_size=1)


#builiding classifier model
cmodel = GaussianNB()


#Creating the model on Training Data
cmodel=cmodel.fit(X_train,y_train)


#input marks for  english, french and mathematics
X_test=[[7,6,8]]


# the predicted result based on the inputs
y_pred=cmodel.predict(X_test)


#print values to the user
print("-------------")
print("Current student's marks as follows:")
```

```
for i in range(len(X_test[0])):

    print(str(i+1)+"."+headers[i],"=", X_test[0][i], " marks")


print("------result-------")
if y_pred[0]=="Yes":
   print("Student will be admitted to the university.")
else:
   print("Student will not be admitted to the university.")


print('Accuracy: ',accuracy_score(y_test,y_pred))
```

Figure 5 Naive Bayes codes

The same codes similar to the one implemented for Logistic Regression had been used here with a single change for the following line of codes:

```
cmodel = GaussianNB()
```

The model used in Example 2 is the Gaussian Naïve Bayes. The same training data and test data used as in Example 1, has purposefully been re-used here to show you a concrete difference in the way the second classifier works to the first.

Different models have different accuracy levels. In Python, when you use the scikit-learn library, as a developer, you will not see the difference. But understanding the different types of models helps to determine the ML techniques you need to use based on the problem you need to solve.

Successful admission

The following output is shown on the user's screen when the input marks were: 7, 6 and 8. The ML program with the Naives Bayes, successfully identified the student as a potential student to the university and print the message *"Student will be admitted to the university"* on the screen.

```
-------------
Current student's marks as follows:
1.ENGLISH = 7  marks
2.FRENCH = 6  marks
3.MATHEMATICS = 8  marks
------result-------
Student will be admitted to the university.
Accuracy:  1.0
```

Figure 6 Successful admission with Naïve Bayes

<u>**Unsuccessful admission**</u>

The following output is shown on the user's screen when the input marks were: 7, 6 and 2. The ML program with the Naives Bayes, identified the student as being ineligible for the admission process. In this case, the following message was printed on screen: *Student will not be admitted to the university.*

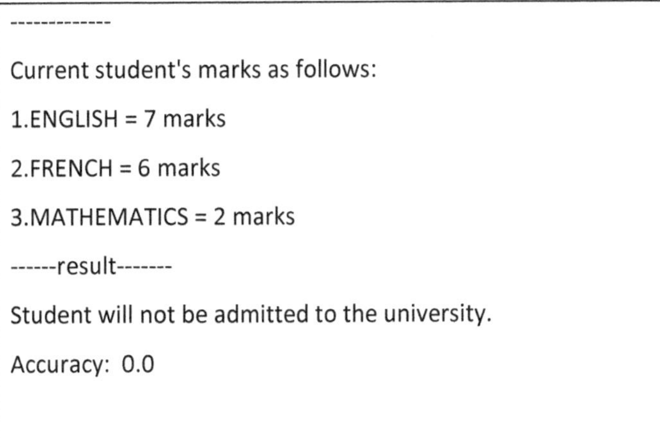

Figure 7 Not eligible for admission with Naïve Bayes

Practical questions

You have learnt about the accuracy score, which is one of the many metrics that exist today for ML. Research on the following metrics:

1.   Precision
2.   Recall
3.   Confusion Matrix
4.   F1 score
5.   Log loss

Example 3: Gaussian Process Classifier

Explanation

Gaussian Processes is based on Laplace approximation, a technique which uses the Gaussian Probability distribution. The Gaussian Processes uses all these different principles combined in its model to perform a prediction.

Gaussian Process (GP) Classifier is a discriminant machine learning model which relies on conditional probability. It uses the Gaussian Probability distribution which forms a bell curve on a map. The points closer to the mean values of the different data points, are more likely to group together rather than those which are far from the mean value, forming an boundary line to separate the two groups: close and far, making GP a discriminant model.

Unlike Logistic Regression and Naives Bayes, which are parametric in nature, Gaussian is a non-parametric function model. This means that the model can dynamically accommodate new dataset and learn accordingly. The model is used for both classification and regression problems.

The following codes show how Gaussian Process has been applied in Python and the steps are explained after the figure.

```python
# import python libraries


from sklearn.gaussian_process import GaussianProcessClassifier
from sklearn.gaussian_process.kernels import RBF
import pandas as pd
import numpy as np
from sklearn.linear_model import LogisticRegression
from sklearn.model_selection import train_test_split


#list of headers/columns
headers=['ENGLISH','FRENCH', 'MATHEMATICS', 'ADMITTED']


# row values
values=[[1, 2, 3, 'No'],
        [3, 4, 5, 'No'],
        [5, 6, 7, 'Yes'],
        [7, 8, 9, 'Yes'],
        [1, 2, 6, 'No'],
        [1, 2, 8, 'No'],
        [3, 5, 5, 'No'],
        [8, 7, 8, 'Yes'],
```

```python
                [7, 7, 7, 'Yes'],
                [8, 2, 5, 'No']])


#Create the frame to include all data and headers
matrix=pd.DataFrame(data=values,columns=headers)



#Separate Target Variable and Predictor Variables
cause=['ENGLISH','FRENCH', 'MATHEMATICS']
effect='ADMITTED'



x=matrix[cause].values
y=matrix[effect].values


#Split the data into training and testing set


X_train, X_test, y_train, y_test = train_test_split(x, y, test_size=l)



#builiding classifier model
cmodel = GaussianProcessClassifier(kernel=RBF())



#Creating the model on Training Data
```

```python
cmodel=cmodel.fit(X_train,y_train)


#input marks for  english, french and mathematics
X_test=[[7,6,8]]


# the predicted result based on the inputs
y_pred=cmodel.predict(X_test)


#print values to the user
print("-------------")
print("Current student's marks as follows:")
for i in range(len(X_test[0])):
    print(str(i+1)+"."+headers[i],"=", X_test[0][i], " marks")


print("------result-------")
if y_pred[0]=="Yes":
   print("Student will be admitted to the university.")
else:
   print("Student will not be admitted to the university.")
```

Figure 8 Gaussian Processes Classifier

The same codes as in Example 1 and Example 2, have been used here with one line being replaced to:

```
cmodel = GaussianProcessClassifier(kernel=RBF())
```

The model used in Example 3 is the Gaussian Process Classifier. The parameter Kernel with value RBF is important to create bias in the values. RBF stands for Radial Bias Function.

Successful admission

The following output is shown on the user's screen when the input marks were: 7, 6 and 8. The ML program with the Gaussian Process Classifier, successfully identified the student as a potential student to the university and print the message *"Student will be admitted to the university"* on the screen.

Current student's marks as follows:

1.ENGLISH = 7 marks

2.FRENCH = 6 marks

3.MATHEMATICS = 8 marks

------result-------

Student will be admitted to the university.

Figure 9 Successfully admission with GP

<u>Unsuccessful admission</u>

The following output is shown on the user's screen when the input marks were: 7, 6 and 2. The ML program with the Gaussian Process Classifier, identified the student as being ineligible for the admission process. The following message was printed on screen: *Student will not be admitted to the university.*

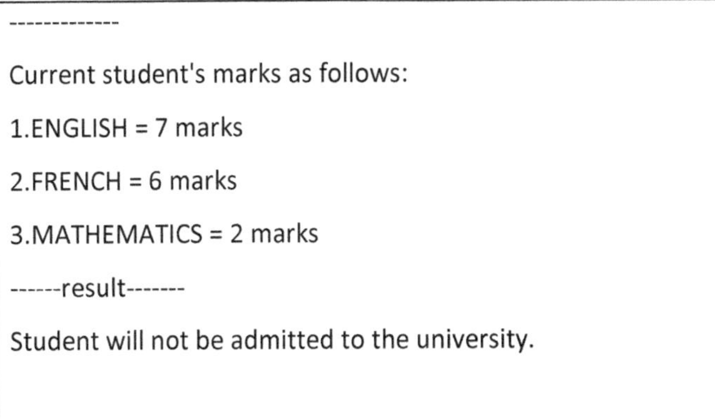

Figure 10 Not eligible for admission with GP

Practical questions

Revise on the following topics:

1. The difference between logistic classifier and regression.
2. The difference between Gaussian Process classifier and Naïve Bayes classifier.
3. The advantages and disadvantages between Logistic Regression and Naïve Bayes classifiers.
4. The formula used for Logistic Regression, Naïve Bayes and Gaussian Process classifier.
5. Difference between accuracy, prediction and recall score in ML.

Example 4: K-Nearest Neighbors (KNN)

Explanation

In the field of statistic, the K-Nearest Neighbors (KNN) was initially developed by Evelyn Fix and Joseph Hodges in 1951, and later enhanced by Thomas Cover (Lopez-Bernal, Balderas, Ponce, & A, 2021). It is both a non-parametric and generative model. It groups data points based on proximity. As it is non-parametric, adding new set of data will not affect the functions used in the model. The non-parametric ability helps the model to adapt dynamically with the new dataset.

The KNN has been used to determine if a new student can be enrolled when his mark is 7, 6 and 8 for thee subjects: English, French and Mathematics. The codes are shown below:

```
import pandas as pd
from sklearn.model_selection import train_test_split
from sklearn.neighbors import KNeighborsClassifier


#list of headers/columns
headers=['ENGLISH','FRENCH', 'MATHEMATICS', 'ADMITTED']


# row values
```

```python
values=[[1, 2, 3, 'No'],
       [3, 4, 5, 'No'],
       [5, 6, 7, 'Yes'],
       [7, 8, 9, 'Yes'],
       [1, 2, 6, 'No'],
       [1, 2, 8, 'No'],
       [3, 5, 5, 'No'],
       [8, 7, 8, 'Yes'],
       [7, 7, 7, 'Yes'],
       [8, 2, 5, 'No']]


#Create the frame to include all data and headers
matrix=pd.DataFrame(data=values,columns=headers)



#Separate Target Variable and Predictor Variables
cause=['ENGLISH','FRENCH', 'MATHEMATICS']
effect='ADMITTED'


x=matrix[cause].values
y=matrix[effect].values


#Split the data into training and testing set


X_train, X_test, y_train, y_test = train_test_split(x, y, test_size=1)
```

```python
#builiding classifier model
cmodel = KNeighborsClassifier()


#Creating the model on Training Data
cmodel=cmodel.fit(X_train,y_train)


#input marks for  english, french and mathematics
X_test=[[7,6,8]]


# the predicted result based on the inputs
y_pred=cmodel.predict(X_test)


#print values to the user
print("-------------")
print("Current student's marks as follows:")
for i in range(len(X_test[0])):
    print(str(i+1)+"."+headers[i],"=", X_test[0][i], " marks")


print("------result-------")
if y_pred[0]=="Yes":
   print("Student will be admitted to the university.")
else:
```

```
print("Student will not be admitted to the university.")
```

Figure 11 KNN codes

The same codes as in previous examples have been used here with one line changed for the KNN model:

```
cmodel = KNeighborsClassifier()
```

<u>**Successful admission**</u>

The following output is shown on the user's screen when the input marks were: 7, 6 and 8. The ML program with the KNN technique, successfully identified the student as a potential student to the university and print the message *"Student will be admitted to the university"* on the screen.

```
-------------
Current student's marks as follows:
1.ENGLISH = 7  marks
2.FRENCH = 6  marks
3.MATHEMATICS = 8  marks
------result-------
Student will be admitted to the university.
```

Figure 12 Successful admission with KNN

<u>**Unsuccessful admission**</u>

The following output is shown on the user's screen when the input marks were: 7, 6 and 2. The ML program with KNN, identified the student as being ineligible for the admission process. The following message was printed on screen: *Student will not be admitted to the university.*

```
--------------

Current student's marks as follows:

1.ENGLISH = 7 marks

2.FRENCH = 6 marks

3.MATHEMATICS = 2 marks

------result-------

Student will not be admitted to the university.
```

Figure 13 Not eligible for admission with KNN

1. The KNN uses the Euclidean distance formula. Research on the relationship created between KNN and Euclidean distance formula.
2. Increase the number of datasets from 10 to 50 and use KNN to find the nearest neighbor points.
3. Plot the points in (2) on a graph.
4. What is the difference between Logistic Regression and KNN?
5. What is the difference between Naïve Bayes (NB) and KNN?

Example 5: Quadratic Discriminant Analysis (QDA)

Explanation

The original discriminant analysis was developed in 1936 by Ronald Fisher (Efron, 2000). The Discriminant Analysis follows a normal distribution alike to the Gaussian Distribution.

The Quadratic Discriminant Analysis (QDA) is used for classification problems, but not for regression problems. It is generative and parametric in nature. The QDA enhances the Linear Discriminant Analysis (LDA) by making it more flexible in its input values (X-values). With LDA, assumption was that X-values should have equal covariances, but with QDA, the latter can cater for unequal covariances.

The QDA has been used to determine if a new student can be enrolled to a university, when his marks were respectively 7, 6 and 8 for the three given subjects: English, French and Mathematics. The codes are shown below:

```python
# import python libraries

import pandas as pd

import numpy as np

from sklearn.model_selection import train_test_split

from sklearn.discriminant_analysis import QuadraticDiscriminantAnalysis


#list of headers/columns

headers=['ENGLISH','FRENCH', 'MATHEMATICS', 'ADMITTED']


# row values

values=[[1, 2, 3, 'No'],

        [3, 4, 5, 'No'],

        [5, 6, 7, 'Yes'],

        [7, 8, 9, 'Yes'],

        [1, 2, 6, 'No'],

        [1, 2, 8, 'No'],

        [3, 5, 5, 'No'],

        [8, 7, 8, 'Yes'],

        [7, 7, 7, 'Yes'],

        [8, 2, 5, 'No']]


values=[[480, 28, 610000, 'Yes'],

        [480, 42, 140000, 'No'],

        [480, 29, 420000, 'No'],
```

```python
       [490, 30, 420000, 'No'],

       [500, 27, 420000, 'No'],

       [510, 34, 190000, 'No'],

       [550, 24, 330000, 'Yes'],

       [560, 34, 160000, 'Yes'],

       [560, 25, 300000, 'Yes'],

       [570, 34, 450000, 'Yes'],

       [590, 30, 140000, 'Yes'],

       [600, 33, 600000, 'Yes'],

       [600, 22, 400000, 'Yes'],

       [600, 25, 490000, 'Yes'],

       [610, 32, 120000, 'Yes'],

       [630, 29, 360000, 'Yes'],

       [630, 30, 480000, 'Yes'],

       [660, 29, 460000, 'Yes'],

       [700, 32, 470000, 'Yes'],

       [740, 28, 400000, 'Yes']]


#Create the frame to include all data and headers
matrix=pd.DataFrame(data=values,columns=headers)



#Separate Target Variable and Predictor Variables
cause=['ENGLISH','FRENCH', 'MATHEMATICS']
effect='ADMITTED'
```

```python
x=matrix[cause].values
y=matrix[effect].values


#Split the data into training and testing set


X_train, X_test, y_train, y_test = train_test_split(x, y, test_size=1)



#builiding classifier model
cmodel = QuadraticDiscriminantAnalysis()



#Creating the model on Training Data
cmodel=cmodel.fit(X_train,y_train)


#input marks for  english, french and mathematics
X_test=[[7,6,2]]


# the predicted result based on the inputs
y_pred=cmodel.predict(X_test)
```

```
#print values to the user
print("-------------")
print("Current student's marks as follows:")
for i in range(len(X_test[0])):
    print(str(i+1)+"."+headers[i],"=", X_test[0][i], " marks")


print("------result-------")
if y_pred[0]=="Yes":
   print("Student will be admitted to the university.")
else:
   print("Student will not be admitted to the university.")
```

Figure 14 QDA codes

The same codes as in previous examples have been used here with one line changed for the QDA model:

```
cmodel = QuadraticDiscriminantAnalysis()
```

Successful admission

The following output is shown on the user's screen when the input marks were: 7, 6 and 8. The ML program with the QDA, successfully identified the student as a potential student to the university and print the message *"Student will be admitted to the university"* on the screen.

```
--------------

Current student's marks as follows:
1.ENGLISH = 7  marks
2.FRENCH = 6  marks
3.MATHEMATICS = 8  marks
------result-------
Student will be admitted to the university.
```

Figure 15 Successful admission with QDA

<u>**Unsuccessful admission**</u>

The following output is shown on the user's screen when the input marks were: 7, 6 and 2. The ML program with QDA, identified the student as being ineligible for the admission process. The following message was printed on screen: *Student will not be admitted to the university.*

```
--------------
```

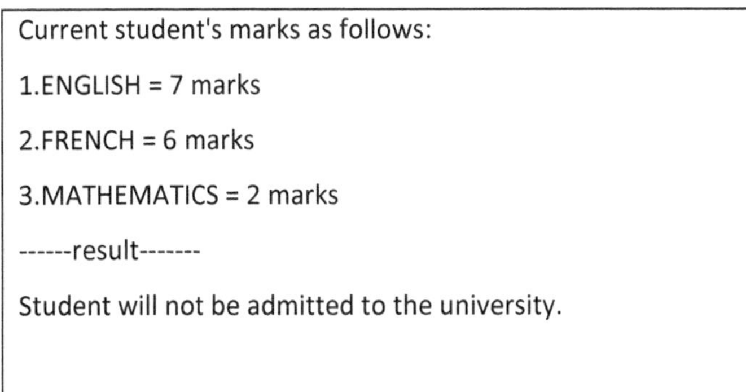

Figure 16 Not eligible for the admission process with QDA

Practical questions

1. Understand the difference between Logistic Regression, Naïve Bayes, and Discriminant models.

2. Two types of discriminant analysis exist. They are the linear and the quadratic discriminant analysis. Provide differences for each of them.

3. Implement the code for linear discriminant analysis in Python.

4. Plot the linear and quadratic discriminant results on a graph.

5. Implement the QDA formula without using the scikit-learn library for your ML program.

Explanation

The first tree classification appeared in the THAID project, by Messenger and Mandell in 1972 (Gepp & Kumar, 2015).

A tree consists of many nodes. It starts with one root node, which is known as the parent node. The latter may have other nodes, and these are known as its child's nodes. Each child can have their own child. A node which does not have any child is known as a leaf node. Looking for the right decision based on the different branches in the tree makes the decision tree a discriminant model. Its decision is always based on a criterion or boundary.

The decision tree is also parametric, meaning its function will not change no matter how many datasets you push to the tree model. Hence, the model is more adapted to small problem.

The decision tree model has been used to determine if a new student can be enrolled to the university, when his marks were respectively 7, 6 and 8 for the three subjects: English, French and Mathematics. The codes are shown below

```python
# import python libraries
import pandas as pd
import numpy as np
from sklearn.tree import DecisionTreeClassifier
from sklearn.model_selection import train_test_split


#list of headers/columns
headers=['ENGLISH','FRENCH', 'MATHEMATICS', 'ADMITTED']


# row values
values=[[1, 2, 3, 'No'],
        [3, 4, 5, 'No'],
        [5, 6, 7, 'Yes'],
        [7, 8, 9, 'Yes'],
        [1, 2, 6, 'No'],
        [1, 2, 8, 'No'],
        [3, 5, 5, 'No'],
        [8, 7, 8, 'Yes'],
        [7, 7, 7, 'Yes'],
        [8, 2, 5, 'No']]


#Create the frame to include all data and headers
matrix=pd.DataFrame(data=values,columns=headers)
```

```python
#Separate Target Variable and Predictor Variables
cause=['ENGLISH','FRENCH', 'MATHEMATICS']
effect='ADMITTED'


x=matrix[cause].values
y=matrix[effect].values


#Split the data into training and testing set


X_train, X_test, y_train, y_test = train_test_split(x, y, test_size=1)


#builiding classifier model
cmodel = DecisionTreeClassifier()


#Creating the model on Training Data
cmodel=cmodel.fit(X_train,y_train)


#input marks for  english, french and mathematics
X_test=[[7,6,8]]


# the predicted result based on the inputs
```

```
y_pred=cmodel.predict(X_test)


#print values to the user
print("-------------")
print("Current student's marks as follows:")
for i in range(len(X_test[0])):
    print(str(i+1)+"."+headers[i],"=", X_test[0][i], " marks")


print("------result-------")
if y_pred[0]=="Yes":
    print("Student will be admitted to the university.")
else:
    print("Student will not be admitted to the university.")
```

Figure 17 Decision Trees codes

The same codes as in previous examples have been used here with one line changed for the decision tree model:

```
cmodel = DecisionTreeClassifier()
```

<u>**Successful admission**</u>

The following output is shown on the user's screen when the input marks were: 7, 6 and 8. The ML program with the decision tree classifier, successfully identified the student as a potential student to the university and print the message *"Student will be admitted to the university"* on the screen.

```
-------------
Current student's marks as follows:
1.ENGLISH = 7  marks
2.FRENCH = 6  marks
3.MATHEMATICS = 8  marks
------result-------
Student will be admitted to the university.
```

Figure 18 Successful admission with decision tree

<u>**Unsuccessful admission**</u>

The following output is shown on the user's screen when the input marks were: 7, 6 and 2. The ML program with KNN, identified the student as being ineligible for the admission process. The following message was printed on screen: *Student will not be admitted to the university.*

```
--------------

Current student's marks as follows:

1.ENGLISH = 7 marks

2.FRENCH = 6 marks

3.MATHEMATICS = 2 marks

------result-------

Student will not be admitted to the university.
```

Figure 19 Not eligible for admission with decision tree

Practical questions

Research on how to:

1. Visualize the tree.

2. Display the Gini index of your tree.

3. Change the existing codes with the following parameters and values:

```
cmodel= DecisionTreeClassifier(criterion='gini',
min_samples_leaf=5, min_samples_split=5, max_depth=None,
random_state=3)
```

4. Analyse the difference in your prediction values.

5. Increase number of dataset and anlyse predicting values.

Example 7: AdaBoost Classifier

Explanation

AdaBoost was modelled by Yoav Freund and Robert Schapire in 1995, who won the 2003 Nobel Prize for their work (Sujatha, Aarthy, Chatterjee, Alaboudi, & Jhanjhi, 2021). AdaBoost, short for Adaptive Boosting, is an ensemble method, which has aim to enhance accuracy of other base models. It is normally used with the decision tree model which is a base model.

The AdaBoosT model has been used to enhance the decision tree in order to determine if a new student can be enrolled to the university, when his marks were 7, 6 and 8 for the three subjects: English, French and Mathematics. The codes are shown below

```python
# import python libraries
import pandas as pd
from sklearn.tree import DecisionTreeClassifier
from sklearn.model_selection import train_test_split
from sklearn.ensemble import AdaBoostClassifier


#list of headers/columns
headers=['ENGLISH','FRENCH', 'MATHEMATICS', 'ADMITTED']
```

```python
# row values
values=[[1, 2, 3, 'No'],
        [3, 4, 5, 'No'],
        [5, 6, 7, 'Yes'],
        [7, 8, 9, 'Yes'],
        [1, 2, 6, 'No'],
        [1, 2, 8, 'No'],
        [3, 5, 5, 'No'],
        [8, 7, 8, 'Yes'],
        [7, 7, 7, 'Yes'],
        [8, 2, 5, 'No']]


#Create the frame to include all data and headers
matrix=pd.DataFrame(data=values,columns=headers)


#Separate Target Variable and Predictor Variables
cause=['ENGLISH','FRENCH', 'MATHEMATICS']
effect='ADMITTED'


x=matrix[cause].values
y=matrix[effect].values
```

```python
#Split the data into training and testing set

X_train, X_test, y_train, y_test = train_test_split(x, y, test_size=1)



#builiding classifier model
dcmodel = DecisionTreeClassifier()
acmodel = AdaBoostClassifier(n_estimators=50, base_estimator=dcmodel
,learning_rate=1)

#Creating the model on Training Data
acmodel=acmodel.fit(X_train,y_train)

#input marks for  english, french and mathematics
X_test=[[7,6,2]]

# the predicted result based on the inputs
y_pred=acmodel.predict(X_test)



#print values to the user
print("-------------")
print("Current student's marks as follows:")
for i in range(len(X_test[0])):
    print(str(i+1)+"."+headers[i],"=", X_test[0][i], " marks")
```

```
print("------result-------")
if y_pred[0]=="Yes":
    print("Student will be admitted to the university.")
else:
    print("Student will not be admitted to the university.")
```

Figure 20 AdaBoost codes

The model used in Example 6 is the Decision Tree Classifier. In Example 7, the same codes as in previous example have been enhanced with one additional line:

```
acmodel = AdaBoostClassifier(n_estimators=50, base_estimator=dcmodel
,learning_rate=1)
```

We want the model to base on a decision tree model first and the parameter base_estimator for the AdaBoostClassifier model has been built.

<u>**Successful admission**</u>

The following output is shown on the user's screen when the input marks were: 7, 6 and 8. The ML program with AdaBoost, successfully identified the student as a potential student to the university and print the message *"Student will be admitted to the university"* on the screen.

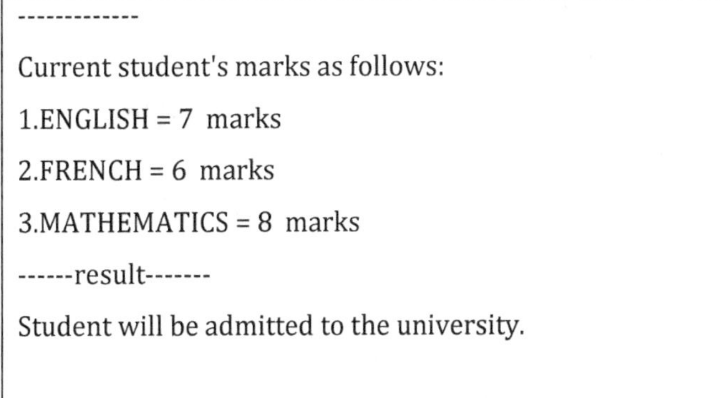

Figure 21 Successful admission with AdaBoost

<u>**Unsuccessful admission**</u>

The following output is shown on the user's screen when the input marks were: 7, 6 and 2. The ML program with AdaBoost, identified the student as being ineligible for the admission process. The following message was printed on screen: *Student will not be admitted to the university.*

Current student's marks as follows:

1.ENGLISH = 7 marks

2.FRENCH = 6 marks

3.MATHEMATICS = 2 marks

------result-------

Student will not be admitted to the university.

Figure 22 Not eligible for admission with AdaBoost

Practical questions

Predict the admission status for students with the following set of marks for English, French and Mathematics:

1. 1,6,3
2. 7,7,7
3. 8,8,8
4. 8,2,8
5. 7,3,4

Example 8: Random Forest Classifier

Explanation

Random Forest classifier acts like the decision tree model with exception that it manages multiple trees. All the different trees will output a result. A vote will be done on these different results so that a final value is pronounced.

In real life, if you wear a pair of shoes, you normally clean your shoes, look for your socks, wear your socks and then finally wear your shoes. In a decision tree, the first action of cleaning the shoes will always be your first decision factor in the model. Some other people can have a different model such as looking for the socks first, then look for the shoes afterwards. Hence, unfortunately, the decision tree model cannot fit for other people's need. In this case, the forest model is more adapted to choose between different models and vote for the most adequate one for that specific person.

The Random Forest model has been used to enhance the decision tree in order to determine if a new student can be enrolled to the university, when his marks were 7, 6 and 8 for the three subjects: English, French and Mathematics. The codes are as shown in the next page:

```python
# import python libraries
import pandas as pd
from sklearn.model_selection import train_test_split
from sklearn.ensemble import RandomForestClassifier


#list of headers/columns
headers=['ENGLISH','FRENCH', 'MATHEMATICS', 'ADMITTED']


# row values
values=[[1, 2, 3, 'No'],
        [3, 4, 5, 'No'],
        [5, 6, 7, 'Yes'],
        [7, 8, 9, 'Yes'],
        [1, 2, 6, 'No'],
        [1, 2, 8, 'No'],
        [3, 5, 5, 'No'],
        [8, 7, 8, 'Yes'],
        [7, 7, 7, 'Yes'],
        [8, 2, 5, 'No']]


#Create the frame to include all data and headers
matrix=pd.DataFrame(data=values,columns=headers)
```

```python
#Separate Target Variable and Predictor Variables
cause=['ENGLISH','FRENCH', 'MATHEMATICS']
effect='ADMITTED'


x=matrix[cause].values
y=matrix[effect].values

#Split the data into training and testing set

X_train, X_test, y_train, y_test = train_test_split(x, y, test_size=1)


#builiding classifier model
cmodel = RandomForestClassifier()


#Creating the model on Training Data
cmodel=cmodel.fit(X_train,y_train)

#input marks for  english, french and mathematics
X_test=[[7,6,8]]
```

```python
# the predicted result based on the inputs
y_pred=cmodel.predict(X_test)



#print values to the user
print("-------------")
print("Current student's marks as follows:")
for i in range(len(X_test[0])):
    print(str(i+1)+"."+headers[i],"=", X_test[0][i]," marks")

print("------result-------")
if y_pred[0]=="Yes":
   print("Student will be admitted to the university.")
else:
   print("Student will not be admitted to the university.")

print('Testing Set Evaluation Accuracy: ',accuracy_score(y_test,y_pred))
```

Figure 23 Random Forest codes

The same codes as in previous examples have been used here with one line changed for the Random Forest model:

cmodel = RandomForestClassifier ()

Successful admission

The following output is shown on the user's screen when the input marks were: 7, 6 and 8. The ML program with the Random Forest, successfully identified the student as a potential student to the university and print the message *"Student will be admitted to the university"* on the screen.

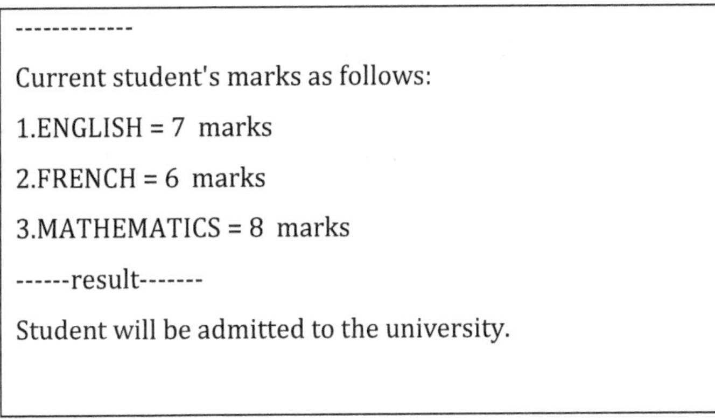

Figure 24 Successful admission with Random Forest

Unsuccessful admission

The following output is shown on the user's screen when the input marks were: 7, 6 and 2. The ML program with Random

Forest, identified the student as being ineligible for the admission process. The following message was printed on screen: *Student will not be admitted to the university.*

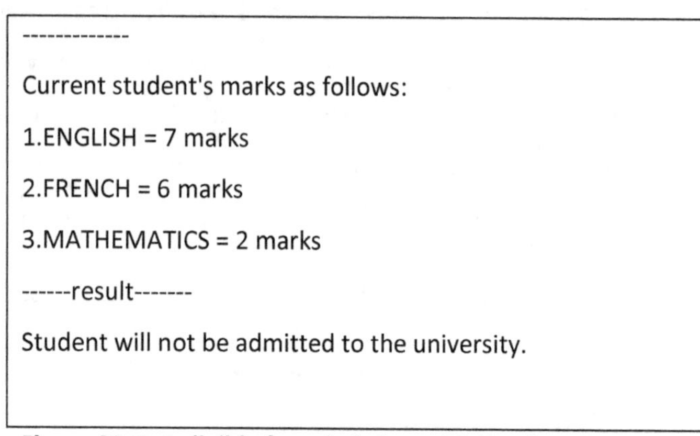

Figure 25 Not eligible for admission with Random Forest

Practical questions

1. Understand the difference between decision Tree and Random Forest classifiers.

2. Implement a random forest tree without using the scikit-learn library.

Example 9: Support Vector Machine (SVM)

Explanation

The original SVM algorithm was invented by Vladimir N. Vapnik and Alexey Ya. Chervonenkis in 1963 (Schölkopf, Burges, & Smola, 1999). It is non-parametric and discriminant model which can solve both classification and regression problem. It can solve complex problem.

The SVM has been used to enhance the decision tree in order to determine if a new student can be enrolled to the university, when his marks were respectively 7, 6 and 8 for the three subjects: English, French and Mathematics. The codes are shown below

```python
# import python libraries
import pandas as pd
from sklearn.model_selection import train_test_split
from sklearn import svm


#list of headers/columns
headers=['ENGLISH','FRENCH', 'MATHEMATICS', 'ADMITTED']


# row values
values=[[1, 2, 3, 'No'],
```

```python
                 [3, 4, 5, 'No'],
                 [5, 6, 7, 'Yes'],
                 [7, 8, 9, 'Yes'],
                 [1, 2, 6, 'No'],
                 [1, 2, 8, 'No'],
                 [3, 5, 5, 'No'],
                 [8, 7, 8, 'Yes'],
                 [7, 7, 7, 'Yes'],
                 [8, 2, 5, 'No']]


#Create the frame to include all data and headers
matrix=pd.DataFrame(data=values,columns=headers)



#Separate Target Variable and Predictor Variables
cause=['ENGLISH','FRENCH', 'MATHEMATICS']
effect='ADMITTED'



x=matrix[cause].values
y=matrix[effect].values


#Split the data into training and testing set


X_train, X_test, y_train, y_test = train_test_split(x, y, test_size=1)
```

```python
#builiding classifier model
cmodel = svm.SVC(kernel='linear')


#Creating the model on Training Data
cmodel=cmodel.fit(X_train,y_train)


#input marks for  english, french and mathematics
X_test=[[7,6,8]]


# the predicted result based on the inputs
y_pred=cmodel.predict(X_test)


#print values to the user
print("-------------")
print("Current student's marks as follows:")
for i in range(len(X_test[0])):
    print(str(i+1)+"."+headers[i],"=", X_test[0][i], " marks")


print("------result-------")
if y_pred[0]=="Yes":
    print("Student will be admitted to the university.")
```

```
else:
    print("Student will not be admitted to the university.")
```

Figure 26 SVM codes

The same codes as in previous examples have been used here with one line changed for the SVM model:

```
cmodel = svm.SVC(kernel='linear')
```

Successful admission

The following output is shown on the user's screen when the input marks were: 7, 6 and 8. The ML program with the SVM, successfully identified the student as a potential student to the university and print the message *"Student will be admitted to the university"* on the screen.

```
-------------
Current student's marks as follows:
1.ENGLISH = 7  marks
2.FRENCH = 6  marks
3.MATHEMATICS = 8  marks
```

------result-------

Student will be admitted to the university.

Figure 27 Successful admission with SVM

<u>**Unsuccessful admission**</u>

The following output is shown on the user's screen when the input marks were: 7, 6 and 2. The ML program with SVM, identified the student as being ineligible for the admission process. The following message was printed on screen: *Student will not be admitted to the university.*

Current student's marks as follows:

1.ENGLISH = 7 marks

2.FRENCH = 6 marks

3.MATHEMATICS = 2 marks

------result-------

Student will not be admitted to the university.

Figure 28 Not eligible for admission with SVM

Practical questions

1. The kernel in an SVM classifier can also be a Radial Basis Function, RBF. Analyse the difference when an RBF is used as your kernel in your codes.
2. Research on how SVM can be used in deep learning, another area of Machine Learning (ML).

Explanation

Multilayer perceptron (MLP) consists of an input, hidden and output layers (Fradkov, 2020). The number of hidden layers determine the accuracy of the model and the dataset inputted.

The perceptron was a machine imitating human neural network. The project to develop the machine was led by Rosenblatt and his team.

The MLP model is discriminant and parametric in nature. Therefore, it is suitable for smaller problems because of its inflexibility nature. However, it can solve both regression and classifications problems.

The perceptron model has been implemented to determine if a new student can be enrolled to the university, when his marks were 7, 6 and 8 for the three subjects: English, French and Mathematics. The codes are shown below

```python
import pandas as pd
from sklearn.model_selection import train_test_split
from sklearn.metrics import accuracy_score
from sklearn.neural_network import MLPClassifier
```

```python
#list of headers/columns
headers=['ENGLISH','FRENCH', 'MATHEMATICS', 'ADMITTED']


# row values
values=[[1, 2, 3, 'No'],
        [3, 4, 5, 'No'],
        [5, 6, 7, 'Yes'],
        [7, 8, 9, 'Yes'],
        [1, 2, 6, 'No'],
        [1, 2, 8, 'No'],
        [3, 5, 5, 'No'],
        [8, 7, 8, 'Yes'],
        [7, 7, 7, 'Yes'],
        [8, 2, 5, 'No']]


#Create the frame to include all data and headers
matrix=pd.DataFrame(data=values,columns=headers)


#Separate Target Variable and Predictor Variables
cause=['ENGLISH','FRENCH', 'MATHEMATICS']
effect='ADMITTED'


x=matrix[cause].values
y=matrix[effect].values
```

```python
#Split the data into training and testing set

X_train, X_test, y_train, y_test = train_test_split(x, y, test_size=1)


#builiding classifier model
cmodel = MLPClassifier(solver='lbfgs',
            alpha=1e-5,
            hidden_layer_sizes=(2,),
            random_state=1)

#Creating the model on Training Data
cmodel=cmodel.fit(X_train,y_train)

#input marks for  english, french and mathematics
X_test=[[7,6,8]]

# the predicted result based on the inputs
y_pred=cmodel.predict(X_test)



#print values to the user
print("-------------")
```

```python
print("Current student's marks as follows:")
for i in range(len(X_test[0])):
    print(str(i+1)+"."+headers[i],"=", X_test[0][i], " marks")


print("------result-------")
if y_pred[0]=="Yes":
    print("Student will be admitted to the university.")
else:
    print("Student will not be admitted to the university.")
```

Figure 29 MLP codes

The same codes as in previous examples have been used here with one line changed for the MLP model:


```python
cmodel = svm.SVC(kernel='linear')
```


<u>**Successful admission**</u>

The following output is shown on the user's screen when the input marks were: 7, 6 and 8. The ML program with the MLP, successfully identified the student as a potential student to the university and print the message *"Student will be admitted to the university"* on the screen.

```
-------------

Current student's marks as follows:

1.ENGLISH = 7  marks

2.FRENCH = 6  marks

3.MATHEMATICS = 8  marks

------result-------

Student will be admitted to the university.
```

Figure 30 Successful admission with MLP

<u>Unsuccessful admission</u>

The following output is shown on the user's screen when the input marks were: 7, 6 and 2. The ML program with MLP, identified the student as being ineligible for the admission process. The following message was printed on screen: *Student will not be admitted to the university.*


```
-------------

Current student's marks as follows:

1.ENGLISH = 7 marks

2.FRENCH = 6 marks
```

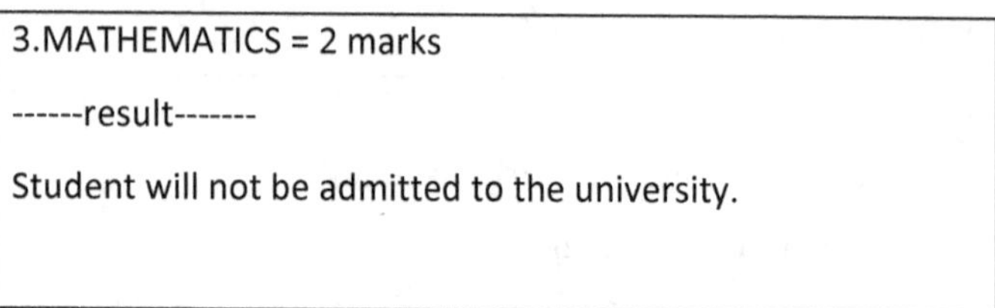

```
3.MATHEMATICS = 2 marks

------result-------

Student will not be admitted to the university.
```

Figure 31 Not eligible for admission with MLP

Practical questions

1. You want to know if a loan would be approved with the following dataset. Write the ML program to predict the new value.

The ML Classification Chart

The following table in the next page, summarises the different classifiers you learnt. The table groups them into the different models: parametric, non-parametric, discriminant, generative models. It also shows the type of probability which is used: joint or conditional probability. In addition, the table shows the type of problems each of these classifiers try to solve.

Table 1 The ML Classification Chart

	Classifier Name	Structural model	Data distribution model	Probability used	Problems solved	Classification or Regression
1.	Logistic Regression (LR)	Parametric	Discriminant	Conditional	Less complex	Both
2.	Naïve Bayes (NB)	Parametric	Generative	Joint	Complex	Classification
3.	Gaussian Process (GP)	Non-Parametric	Discriminant	Conditional	Less complex	Classification
4.	K-Nearest Neighbors (KNN)	Non-Parametric	Generative	Joint	Complex	Classification
5.	Quadratic Discriminant Analysis (QDA)	Parametric	Generative	Joint	Less complex	Classification
6.	Decision Trees Classifier	Parametric	Discriminant	Conditional	Less complex	Classification
7.	AdaBoost Classifier	Parametric	Discriminant	Conditional	Less complex	Classification
8.	Random Forest	Parametric	Discriminant	Conditional	Less complex	Classification
9.	Support Vector Machine (SVM)	Non-Parametric	Discriminant	Conditional	Less complex	Both
10.	Multiple Perceptron (MLP)	Parametric	Discriminant	Conditional	Less complex	Both

References

Arthur, J. (2012). *Research Methods and Methodologies in Education.* SAGE Publications Ltd.

Berrar, D. (2018). Bayes' theorem and naive Bayes classifier. Encyclopedia of Bioinformatics and Computational Biology. *ABC of Bioinformatics, 403.*

Bird, T., & Cassell, J. (2014). *Brilliant Selling (Brilliant Business)* (2 edition ed.). Pearson.

Books, C. (2015). *New 2015 A-Level Business: AQA Year 1 & AS Complete Revision & Practice.* Coordination Group Publications Ltd.

Books, C. (2015). *New 2015 A-Level Business: AQA Year 1 & AS Complete Revision & Practice.* Coordination Group Publications Ltd.

Brown, R. E. (2016). Hebb and Cattell: the genesis of the theory of fluid and crystallized intelligence. *Frontiers in human neuroscience*, 606.

Bryman, A. (2012). *Social Research Methods* (4 edition ed.). OUP Oxford.

Clark, T., Osterwalder, A., & Pigneur, Y. (2012). *Business Model You: A One-Page Method For Reinventing Your Career* (1 edition ed.). John Wiley & Sons.

Cooper, M. (2012). *Financial Times Guide to Business Development: How to Win Profitable Customers and Clients (The FT Guides)* (1 edition ed.). Financial Times/ Prentice Hall.

Dibb, S. (2010). *The Market Segmentation Workbook: Target Marketing for Marketing Managers (Marketing Workbooks).* Cengage Learning.

Duhigg, C. (2013). *The Power of Habit: Why We Do What We Do, and How to Change.* Random House Books.

Efron, B. (2000). RA Fisher in the 21st Century I. In Statistics for the 21st Century. *In Statistics for the 21st Century,* pp. 25-76.

Evans, V. (2013). *FT Essential Guide to Developing a Business Strategy: How to Use Strategic Planning to Start Up or Grow Your Business (Financial Times Series)* (1 edition ed.). FT Publishing International.

Felton, G. (2013). *Advertising: Concept and Copy* (3rd Revised edition edition ed.). W. W. Norton & Company.

Fleming, G. (2011). 12 Top Tips if you are using an NEC Contract. *AIS*, 3.

Fradkov, A. L. (2020). Early history of machine learning. *IFAC-PapersOnLine, 53*(2), 1385-1390.

Fripp, G. (2015). *Market Segmentation Study Guide.* Geoff Fripp.

Gepp, A., & Kumar, K. (2015). Predicting financial distress: A comparison of survival analysis and decision tree techniques. *Procedia Computer Science, 54,* 396-404.

Global Advertising Lawyers Alliance. (2015). *Alcohol Advertising: A Global Legal Perspective: Second Edition* (2 edition ed.). CreateSpace Independent Publishing Platform.

Holliday, N. (2011). *Internet Marketing for Plumbers: Advertising and Marketing Your Plumbing Company Online Using a Website, Google, Facebook, YouTube, Angie's List, LinkedIn, Search Engine Optimization, and More!* CreateSpace Independent Publishing Platform.

Joyner, M., & Borgenicht, D. (2012). *The Worst-Case Scenario Business Survival Guide* ([Large Print] edition ed.). ReadHowYouWant.

Judkins, R. (2015). *The Art of Creative Thinking.* Sceptre.

Kennedy, A. (2015). *Business Development For Dummies* (1 edition ed.). John Wiley & Sons.

Kim, W., & Mauborgne, R. (2015). *Blue Ocean Strategy, Expanded Edition* (Expanded edition edition ed.). Harvard Business Review Press.

King, J. (2015). *Conspiracy Theories: A Guide to the World's Most Intriguing Mysteries.* Summersdale.

Kitchen, M., & Ivanescu, Y. (2015). *Profitable Social Media Marketing: How To Grow Your Business Using Facebook, Twitter, Instagram, LinkedIn And More* (2 edition ed.). CreateSpace Independent Publishing Platform.

Kothari, C. (2012). *Research Methodology :: Methods and Techniques.* New Age International Pvt Ltd Publishers.

Kumar, R. (2014). *Research Methodology: A Step-by-Step Guide for Beginners* (Fourth Edition edition ed.). SAGE Publications Ltd.

Larmour, J. (2011). *Interdisciplinary Design for the Built Environment.* London: the master thesis.

Latham, M. (1994). *Constructing the Team.* London : HMSO.

Lewis, D. D. (1998). Naive (Bayes) at forty: The independence assumption in information retrieval. *European conference on machine learning* (pp. pp. 4-15). Springer, Berlin, Heidelberg.

Lopez-Bernal, D., Balderas, D., Ponce, P., & A, M. (2021). Education 4.0: teaching the basics of KNN, LDA and simple perceptron algorithms for binary classification problems. Future Internet. *Future Internet, 13*(8).

Markandeya, S., & Roy, K. (2014). *SAP ABAP: Hands-On Test Projects with Business Scenarios* (2014 edition ed.). Apress.

McDonald, M. (2012). *Market Segmentation: How to Do it and How to Profit from it* (Revised 4th Edition edition ed.). John Wiley & Sons.

Mckeown, M. (2015). *The Strategy Book (2nd Edition)* (2 edition ed.). FT Publishing International.

Meng, X. (2012). International Journal of Project Management. *The effect of relationship management on project performance in construction, 30*(2), 188-198.

Murdoch, J., & Hughes, W. (2007). *Construction Contracts Law and management* (4th ed.). London and New York: Taylor&Francis.

Nigel, S. (2002). *Engineering Project Management* (2nd ed.). London: Blackwell Publishing.

Osterwalder, A., & Pigneur, Y. (2010). *Business Model Generation: A Handbook for Visionaries, Game Changers, and Challengers* (1 edition ed.). John Wiley & Sons.

RICS. (2013). *Developing a construction procurement strategy and selecting an appropriate route.* London: the Royal Institution of Chartered Surveyors.

Saritas, M. M., & Yasar, A. (2019). Performance analysis of ANN and Naive Bayes classification algorithm for data classification. *International Journal of Intelligent Systems and Applications in Engineering, 7*(2), 88-91.

Scheessele, W. (2012). *60 Insights for Mastering Business Development.* CreateSpace Independent Publishing Platform.

Schölkopf, B., Burges, C. J., & Smola, A. J. (1999). Advances in kernel methods: support vector learning. *MIT press.*

Sharp, B. (2010). *How Brands Grow: What Marketers Don't Know.* Oxford University Press.

Smith, M. (2014). *Targeted: How Technology Is Revolutionizing Advertising and the Way Companies Reach Consumers.* Amacom.

Struhl, D. (2013). *Market Segmentation: An Introduction and Review* (1 edition ed.). CreateSpace Independent Publishing Platform.

Sujatha, R., Aarthy, S. L., Chatterjee, J., Alaboudi, A., & Jhanjhi, N. Z. (2021). A machine learning way to classify autism spectrum disorder. *International Journal of Emerging Technologies in Learning (iJET), 16*(6), 182-200.

Surridge, M., & Gillespie, A. (2015). *AQA Business for A Level 1 (Surridge & Gillespie) (AQA A Level Business)*. Hodder Education.

Williams, S. (2015). *The Financial Times Guide to Business Start Up 2016: The Most Comprehensive Annually Updated Guide for Entrepreneurs (The FT Guides)* (1 edition ed.). FT Publishing International.

Zutshi, S. (2015). *Property Magic: How To Buy Property Using Other People's Time, Money And Experience* (5 edition ed.). Panoma Press.